SEARCHENEERING
TEN Steps to Finding the **PERFECT** JOB

ISBN: 1490563350
ISBN-13: 9781490563350

Visit www.booksurge.com to order additional copies.

SEARCHENEERING
TEN Steps to
Finding the
PERFECT JOB

Carolyn Thompson

I hate to burst your bubble here on page one, but there is no perfect job!

Sure, sometimes a job or a company seems perfect for you. But once you get there, you might find that the people working there don't seem to have it all together. Or vice versa, you might discover a job description that wasn't that interesting to read is actually a great job based on the people who are on the team.

The good news is that there are a lot of worthwhile jobs with excellent potential out there. It's possible to find a job that is as close as it can be to perfect, but you really have to look for it since it's highly unlikely that it will miraculously find you. This book intends to lay out multiple, executable strategies that will enable you to engineer your job search strategy so you can find that elusive opportunity that blends not only your experience and skills but also your interests.

If you have prepared your resume in accordance with *RESUMAZING - Ten Easy Steps To A Perfect Resume,* you are ready to start the job search process. Before we move forward it's important to realize some universal truths about searching for a job.

- Finding a great job is more about timing than anything else. A company has to either be actively or passively looking for someone with your expertise. This can be a moving target because maybe a company you have identified as one you would really like to work for doesn't need someone with your expertise at this time. It can take months for something to open up, so you need to be strategic in how you approach a job search.

- Ideally, you don't want to look for a job when you are desperate for work because taking a job to pay the bills and making a strategic career move are two very different things.

- The easiest way to find a great job requires a blended approach using a combination of modern technology and old-school research techniques. It's impossible for any company to advertise all the openings they have at any given time. Advertising is expensive and the number of unqualified candidates applying to jobs posted on the Internet is unbelievably high. The Internet has made information more available to job seekers but also makes the process more tedious, as not all posted openings are current. Company websites and job search engines are helpful but they often contain stale, inaccurate information. Use them in your research, but be aware that seven out of ten positions you are applying for are either nearing the end of the search process, already filled internally, or the job requirements have been up- or downgraded based on market conditions.

- Be specific and honest about salary, annual cash bonus, any signing bonuses you have received, and actual used value of tuition reimbursement. All these items are verifiable by future employers in a variety of ways: your annual tax returns, payroll tax deposits made on your behalf by the company, and your credit score/rating. Even counselors at the unemployment office can see in a matter of a few clicks how much money you made based on how much payroll tax has been paid on your behalf.

- The most successful job seekers set a schedule for themselves in order to accomplish all the work that needs to happen each week during their job search. When setting your calendar, take into account all the activities that need to happen: you need to network, conduct Internet research, make phone calls, attend events and meetings, schedule interviews, and prepare correspondence among other things. Coordinating the appropriate blend of activities that makes the best use of your available time is the key to creating a productive, successful agenda for yourself. Set aside time on both workdays and weekends — at the correct time of day — to perform the work when it's most appropriate. For instance, you can't reserve time to call people over the weekend who are only reachable during normal business hours. Internet research, though, can be done on evenings and weekends thereby reserving traditional work hours for interacting with businesspeople you need to reach.

Before sending out your resume, try this quick pre-search litmus test:

- What kind of work do I want to do?

  - Based on your resume preparation you should have already identified what you like to do and what you want to do in a new role. We are talking about actual work that you will be paid to perform; your hard, measurable skills.

- What's important to you in your next company?

  - Is it the commute? Is it social responsibility? Is it a casual dress code? Benefits? These are all characteristics that are not generally flexible so you need to be honest with yourself about what you're looking for that's non-negotiable. Either a company offers what you want or they don't. You will not be the person they hire who changes everything for everyone else. Considering these issues up front will increase your chances of finding a good cultural and intellectual fit with the other staff, because the company will attract like-minded people based on the culture they have created.

Your future employer will be paying you to do a job; you will not be paying them, so keep in mind that items like work/life balance and job security don't come from a list of benefits like flex time, telecommuting, or a strong 401(k) plan. These items, particularly, come from within yourself; they're not something anyone else can offer you. Personal security and satisfaction stem from your ability to be organized. With thoughtful effort, anyone can manage personal and family responsibilities, keep professional skills fresh, and continually network within an industry and personal business community.

Whether you are a recent college grad, an experienced professional or perhaps even post retirement looking for part-time work to keep busy, anyone can employ these job search strategies and come out a winner in the end. You may use all ten steps or only one or two, but it's the combination of these tips that will ultimately result in your receiving an offer of employment, one you really want and will excel in, because it's doing work you truly enjoy.

Understanding The Process

Even though the world and its processes are automated, it's still an individual or a group of people who will hire you. Finding a job requires not only determination and skills but also effective, professional communication and follow-up to ultimately be the one who receives the coveted offer letter.

Your goal in sending out your resume should be to reach the decision maker as soon as possible, ideally first. If you can avoid placing yourself in the pile of all the other resumes, you are one step ahead of the game.

Whenever possible, try to communicate with the final decision maker without circumventing the proper recruiting protocol. If you can identify who your future boss might be, reach out to him or her. You can inform this person of your qualifications and interest in the position and ask for guidance through the proper channels to receive an invitation to interview.

Starting at the top and working your way back through the recruiting process will give you a lot of information that you cannot get by simply responding to ads. Communicating with managers first will ensure that you are, in fact, submitting your resume for a viable position. These people will understand what work you have done and furthermore they will know if there is a current or future need for someone like you.

Getting names of people who are decision makers in a certain department can be a challenge but generally worthwhile in the end.

You can use company websites or social and professional networking sites such as LinkedIn to search for names of people who already work at the company you are targeting. You can also ask friends, neighbors, colleagues, and family members for referrals of people that they might know who work there. The human resources department, while very useful after you become an employee, will generally not provide you any information like this while you conduct your job search.

After obtaining a qualified name or two, call the main number of the company and ask for the person by name. Introduce yourself, tell the person how you got his or her name, and ask for the person's assistance in navigating the process. Find out who the manager or decision maker is in the department or area that interests you.

This can be a daunting task for someone who has never done it, so here is a scenario about how that conversation might unfold when calling the main number:

"Can you connect me to Joe Smith, please?"

"Hello, this is Joe Smith."

"Joe, hello, my name is Carolyn Thompson, and I found your name on LinkedIn. I need your help— do you have a minute?"

"Sure, Carolyn, how can I help you?"

"Well, I am very interested in working at your company. I saw on LinkedIn that you are a director in the customer care area and I am looking for a position as a manager in that or a closely related department. By any chance, are there any positions like this open now?"

Listen to what the person has to say.

- If there are no openings, ask if you can send a copy of your resume by e-mail for future consideration. If the person tells you to send it through the company website or human resources department, agree to do so, but you should also ask if you can send it to him or her directly to share your background with other colleagues as the person sees fit.

- If there is a current opening, don't launch into a lengthy presentation of yourself. These people are busy executives and have only a minute or so to chat. You also run the risk of highlighting areas of your expertise they are not interested in. Instead, politely inquire what they might be looking for. If you are a fit (meaning you have at least 75 percent of what the employer is looking for), then ask if the person would consider taking a look at your resume to see if there is anything you should emphasize before applying.

Even though you have gotten a leg up on the process from an internal referral, it's essential to follow the proper channels to ultimately be hired. Human Resources, Talent Acquisition, or Recruiting may need to be involved for EEOC reporting or other reasons so follow the process the person tells you the company has set forth. He or she is also a great source of corporate information so make sure your interaction is positive and professional.

Whether you are referred, apply online, or are presented by a recruiter, you will have to fill out applications and paperwork, much of which is now online. It can be a tedious process because each company you pursue has customized forms; you can't cut and paste the information. Having the necessary information at your fingertips is extremely helpful.

Key items to have ready include:

- Your salary history—broken down as salary plus bonus. Don't inflate the numbers, as most companies verify this information at some point, often after you are already working there. The fine print on the application usually states that you understand providing inaccurate information may be cause for dismissal.

- Your actual dates of employment—including months. If you were a consultant or a temporary employee, you must note that on the application; otherwise, the company cannot properly verify the information. Many employment verifications are done by computerized searches now so make sure whoever the actual paycheck came from is noted as the employer. My company, for instance, employs many contract consultants and temporary employees at a variety of large companies such as Sprint, Verizon, and Accenture. An example of how this information might read is as follows:

Sprint, Overland Park, Kansas (through COMPANY NAME)
1/2007–12/2008
Senior Financial Analyst

- <u>Your reference list</u>—you should have two former supervisors, a peer, a subordinate, and perhaps an associate or outside vendor you have a business relationship with. Friends and family members are never appropriate. Professors and instructors are appropriate only when you are a recent college (or high school) graduate. Make sure these people have given you permission to use them as references. It's important that you offer current daytime contact information since anyone who may be checking references will be working during the day, not evening. Letting your references know that they may be contacted may help to speed the process as they will be expecting a call from an unknown number.

- <u>Your job descriptions and accomplishments</u>—these should be on your resume already but you need to be prepared to type this information into an application if asked. Many times the application is as much a test of your ability to communicate in writing as it is a way to send information to the end user. Even though you really want to type "see resume," try not to. You never know who in the hiring process is looking at what screen when, so try to convey—in a couple of quick sentences—accurate answers to the questions asked.

- <u>Additional information</u>—if you have a job that requires writing articles, public speaking, or if you have won accolades on specialized topics, you should have an addendum prepared separate from your resume for presenting this information. Legal, medical, biomedical, writing, editing, accounting, and various other professionals are often asked to provide a list of published articles. Preparing this information as an addendum to your resume will make updating it easier as time progresses. It will also make it easier for you to offer a copy to interested parties when they request it instead of using up a lot of space for it in your initial resume submission.

STEP TWO:

Customized Searching

When conducting a confidential, strategic, career-oriented job search, responding to Internet postings is enhanced by your ability to perform customized research.

There are three ways to search and identify possible places of employment:

- Geography

- Industry

- Skills

Finding companies in your area that might need your knowledge and skills requires you to sort through your resume and make a list of keywords in the following areas:

- Specific expertise and certifications you have acquired

- Technical skills you offer

- Industry knowledge you possess

Choose three Internet job search websites that you will use for research. These sites vary widely and their popularity is based on your location as well as your industry. Perform searches in your geographic area with your individual keywords. Indeed, Simply Hired, Monster, and CareerBuilder may have some overlap, but we are NOT searching for job titles here. You want to use the extensive amount of database information that is available to you as a job searcher to create a list of companies located in your geographic area that employ people with your skills and expertise.

Remember, this is all about timing. These companies may not necessarily be actively advertising immediate positions that grab your attention, but it would be logical to assume that they would be highly likely to have a need for you at some point based on your unique skills and experience. For example, companies that advertise openings for SAP programmers also may need managers, directors, and other people with SAP skills, but advertising costs and timing may prohibit them from posting a specific position that's perfect for you at the exact time you happen to be looking for one.

The following worksheet is an example of a way to organize your job search research notes. You may choose to create your own spreadsheet or list, but it's important to organize yourself from the start.

Keywords			
Geography	Industry Knowledge	Skills	Certifications/ Other

Companies to look into			

> Marketing Plan: I would report to someone titled _____ or possibly _____. Search online databases, my contacts, and www.LinkedIn.com for people with those titles at these companies to contact. MAKE A LIST AND TRACK INFORMATION GATHERED.

GEOGRAPHIC SEARCH

For positions under the C, V, and D levels (CEO, CFO, COO, VP, Director) most employers want to hire a local person if at all possible. Hiring locally enables companies to avoid the high cost of relocation as well as allowing them to hire someone already rooted in the community who is more likely to stay in their position longer.

Geography can be broken down even further to include commute. As gas prices continue to fluctuate and generally rise, shorter commutes become more and more attractive both personally and financially.

Decide where you want to live as well as where you are willing to commute. Most professionals commute between thirty and sixty minutes each way. In larger metropolitan areas, it can be as long as ninety minutes inclusive of train connections, etc.

Using a map, identify a zip code in your desired area and use it for researching companies located in or near that area. Enter the zip code without any other parameters into one of your selected research sites. You will be surprised how many names of companies (potential employers) pop up that you would not find by simply searching job titles. Most people search by job title only when looking for a new job, thus neglecting to fully utilize the available database information.

List the companies that pique your interest by name on your worksheet.

INDUSTRY SEARCH

In the same manner you used for zip code, search your area using industry keywords. List those companies on your worksheet in a separate column. You may start to see the same companies coming up more than once at this point.

SKILLS SEARCH

Again, use your worksheet and search using your expertise, technical skills, and certification keywords.

Specific expertise refers to areas within your industry that reflect your experience. As an accountant, maybe you have international consolidations experience. As a technical professional perhaps you have SQL or global template experience. A marketing professional might have business development and branding experience. As a paralegal maybe you have mergers and acquisitions experience.

Technical skills include software, hardware, and other technical requirements specific to your industry.

For certifications, you want to list only those that are appropriate for the work you intend to perform.

Now, list the companies you find looking for people with your skills and certifications.

By now you are probably unable to control your desire to click through and read the job descriptions you are finding posted along the way in this exercise, but try to print those out for later use and fully complete your research process first.

Now that you have a useful list of companies that would need someone with your expertise located in your geographic area, you need to find supervisors at these companies to contact. Think about:

- Whom would you report to?

- What is the person's title?

- What is the title of his or her boss?

This is all the information necessary for you to gather names to contact. Your prospective boss has peers elsewhere and they will know if the company has a current or future need for someone with your background. These individuals will also know other colleagues who may be helpful to you. Researching people by job title and company name on LinkedIn will generate an amazing list of people currently working or who have previously worked at the companies on your list. These people are most likely decision makers or they know who is.

Do you personally know anyone currently working at any of the companies on your list? If so, ask him or her to help you find the name of the person you might report to at their company—ultimately your potential new boss. Discuss with your acquaintance what titles the decision makers for the company might have and in what departments they may be located. If your friend knows the person you need to contact, would he or she be willing to drop off a hard copy of your resume? Your friend may direct you to apply through human resources, advice you will gratefully acknowledge, but kindly request help to ascertain who the final decision maker is. Remember, when finding the perfect job, you need to contact the decision maker whenever possible. Even the boss one level above can be very helpful to you because that person can pass your resume to whomever they deem appropriate.

When first contacting these people, you can e-mail your resume with a note, or you can send it via express US Postal Service mail to make sure it gets to the person's desk and is not simply deleted from his or her inbox. Very few people get anything by mail anymore in the office. When the nearly empty mail cart comes around the corner with an envelope bearing your resume being personally delivered to your possible future boss, it will be a welcome diversion in the person's day, not just another e-mail to deal with. Besides, it can be difficult to obtain someone's e-mail address but you can always use Express Mail for just a few dollars at the post office.

Whether you e-mail or snail mail your resume, the cover letter you include when sending an unsolicited resume needs to be short and sweet and include the major highlights of why you are contacting the person:

> Enclosed is my resume for your consideration. I am very interested in working for your company and think my skill set and industry experience make me a good candidate for a position in your department.
>
> I appreciate your advance consideration of my background and look forward to your feedback soon. I can be reached most days on my cell phone (xxx) xxx-xxxx.
>
> Thank you for your time, and have a great day.

You can add a bit more detail such as if you were referred by another employee that this person knows, or perhaps something newsworthy and pertinent to the reader. You shouldn't include salary information or set forth any expectation of a meeting. If you intend to follow up with a call, let the person know that. Make sure you actually make the call when you say you will; otherwise, you will fall short of an expectation you didn't need to set. Besides, you can call them anytime you want; you don't have to tell them anything like that in your letter.

If you don't hear anything within a week or two, you should follow up. If you call, you'll most likely get voice mail. Leave a message stating your name and say that you sent your resume and were hoping for some feedback. Don't forget to leave the phone number and e-mail address where the person can contact you. Provide the same information if you e-mail. Calling before or after common work hours will almost ensure you reach a dial by name directory rather than an actual person answering the phone. This enables you to reach their voicemail faster than possibly being screened by someone paid specifically to screen that person's calls.

Now, if you get your targeted decision maker on the phone, be courteous. Thank him or her for reviewing your resume and ask for feedback. Ask what positions the company might have open now as well as in the near future. Request referrals to internal colleagues and decision makers they might know of at other companies. This is also a good time for you to follow up about his or her department.

Here's an example of how a conversation like this might go:

"Mr. Smith, this is Susan Stewart. I recently forwarded my resume to your attention. Do you have a moment?"

"Yes, Ms. Stewart, but I'm due in a meeting in five minutes. How can I help you?"

"I sent my resume to your attention a few weeks ago because I would like to work for your company. Several people I have spoken with suggested that you might need someone like me in your department, and, if not, that you might be able to recommend other colleagues who might be looking to hire someone with my skill set. Have you had a chance to review my qualifications?"

"Yes, and we will need someone with your background in the next few months, but not at this time."

"I appreciate that. Would it be alright if I follow up with you in a couple of months about the specific position?"

"Yes, sure, check back in about eight to ten weeks. I should have the position approved by then and you can formally submit your resume at that time."

"I'll do that, and I look forward to continuing our dialogue in the future. Have a nice day and thanks very much for your time."

You should always send a thank you note for his or her time, regardless of the outcome of your conversation. E-mail or standard mail is fine for this type of communication.

Networking

Since over 80 percent of new jobs are obtained through personal referrals or networking, this is probably the most important step. You've already identified the key companies in your area that are looking for people with your skills and expertise, so let's find people you know to help you get in there.

Personal referrals are great. If you get a job because of a referral from someone you know you will already have a friendly colleague at your new company. Ask your friends and colleagues to think beyond their current employer as well. Even if your acquaintance left a company in the past, that doesn't mean you should avoid that company. People leave companies and jobs for a wide variety of reasons. Individual departments at the same company can be drastically dissimilar so your employment experience with any given employer could be 180 degrees different from what your friend experienced. Remember, you've done a lot of research into where you may be a fit, and you should welcome any avenue you find to explore those companies further.

Professional associations and industry groups are terrific places to meet people who work at your target companies and many offer career-specific certifications. You should pursue any and all opportunities for continuing education and leadership positions in these groups.

Alumni organizations and community groups offer fun and useful venues where you can meet people you wouldn't have had the opportunity to encounter in other circumstances.

Every city has business networking events run by the chamber of commerce, schools of continuing education, newspapers and employers in the area. This is a great way to meet a large cross section of people. These types of events are often frequented by executive search firms and recruiters because they consider them a good use of their time in order to meet a lot of people in person at one time. As a job seeker, take these chances to meet these recruiters too.

Any chance to make a first impression with someone is a door that can open for you. Many companies list charity events they sponsor on their website. You can volunteer to work the registration table or participate in the event to meet current company employees. Industry conferences or local career fairs also afford you the opportunity to network directly with target company employees who may be able to refer you internally.

No matter what events you attend, participation will get you farther than just showing up. Be prepared to both offer and collect business cards and take some notes if you need to. Sometimes people don't bring their cards so you will need to write down their information in order to reach out to them later. It only takes one job offer so even though you may not glean what you wanted from the first event, don't give up. Attending once won't likely garner you long lasting relationships, but getting more involved and attending regularly, perhaps even volunteering your time will result in creating connections with people you wouldn't have met otherwise.

Depending on your market and skillset, you should attend an event a minimum of once a week. In larger cities, two to three events a week is not out of the question. You can supplement these efforts with virtual networking using LinkedIn groups.

If you haven't registered on LinkedIn (www.LinkedIn.com), you should do it now. LinkedIn and other social networking sites are full of information and people to contact in your job search. Think logically about whom you connect with and invite to be on your list. People you worked with previously, who have similar skill sets to yours but have moved on to other companies, may have a good list of contacts for you to utilize on their LinkedIn profiles. Once you register and log in, invite as many professionals as you can who are in your industry. Inviting people at your current company may open up lists of contacts at their previous employers as well. Having this data available to you is important when it comes to finding the right name to contact about directing your resume to the specific department head.

Don't be afraid to reach out to people on LinkedIn. You can call the main number at any company, ask for the person, and say you found him or her on LinkedIn. Then ask the person for help. I get these calls all the time. You can e-mail people through the site as well, but it costs extra. No contact information is available on the site unless you are connected directly to the person, so you will have to look it up, but if you have been taking active notes along the way, you probably printed out the company's website with the main number on it.

Participating in virtual groups is one of the main attractions on LinkedIn. Paid employment advertising is available but many people post job opportunities under the discussion tabs on groups so the more groups you join, the more notifications you will receive. You can control your email frequency for all your groups through the settings. Some people like daily notifications, some prefer a weekly digest, and others don't want emails at all but would rather monitor the activities live. This can be time consuming if you are in a lot of large groups but the larger the group, the more leads you will likely find.

One important point about networking – you need to feed the machine continually, not just when it's important to you, because networking is a two way street. Take the chance while you are in need of help to expand your network to help others expand theirs as well. Introducing people to each other who might be able to team on projects, do business with each other or giving job leads to other job seekers will garner you more referrals in return.

After you find a job, you need to keep networking. Maybe not at the same pace as when you were job seeking, but attending these events a minimum of once a month will help keep yourself relevant and continue to nurture your networking relationships. Taking a committee or board leadership role is a great way to develop stronger relationships with people and get to know them better. It's easier to receive referrals when people know you, so take charge of your networking plan and get involved professionally.

Responding To Ads And Websites

There are a lot of good jobs out there and modern technology makes it really easy to send your resume to multiple postings, but be mindful of the signal that sends to the screener on the other end. You could unknowingly be telling people something about yourself that you don't want them to think by applying to multiple positions within the same company. Yes, it's possible that there are multiple positions you are qualified for, but if you think you are a long shot for a job, don't apply. Choose wisely, and consider your appropriate level; apply only to exactly what you are qualified for, not for a promotion or a step back. Read the job descriptions; if they ask for three to five years of experience, that's what they want. If you have ten, you are probably overqualified and it's highly likely that job will not pay you what you want.

At many companies, even large ones, people in the recruiting department are very close-knit and they discuss what they are doing with each other. Also, your resume is likely loading into a database there for all the recruiters to access. Conversely, there are times when a recruiter will find your resume in his or her database and call you about a job. This is an in for you. Get the person's name, treat him or her with respect, and offer to send a fresh copy of your resume by e-mail. It's hard to get e-mail addresses, so if someone calls you, make the most of it. Make a great impression and don't hold it against a person who is less experienced in his or her job. Recruiters have a career path to follow too, so be understanding.

If you are sending personalized e-mails or cover letters and you prepare them in a mass mailing, make sure you have the right names, job titles, company names, etc. on the letters and e-mails before they go out. I'd estimate that 40 percent of letters and correspondence prepared in mass mailings are erroneous; make sure you check it carefully before you send it. It will get tossed if the company name is wrong; attention to detail is important.

When responding to ads and website postings, assume the initial reader of your resume has most likely never done the same work as you and, possibly, has no idea what you do, but instead was hired to perform keyword searches and gather initial information. Internal recruiters are hired to prescreen people and they are crucial to the hiring process. First impressions count here so even if the recruiter asks you questions that seem irrelevant, be professional, provide the information he or she is asking for, and make sure you are direct and honest about your pay. Don't avoid the question or be vague in your answer, and don't toss out a blended number of your salary and bonus combined. Combining the numbers could knock you out of the running by putting you over the intended salary range. Answer factually about your current or most recent salary, plus cash bonus; if you are open to a pay cut, let the recruiter know that. Don't state a salary range you are looking for at this point, as you could also sell yourself short here without even knowing it. Instead, ask the recruiter what the range is, and say you are looking in that range (if you are).

Many companies do not want to make job offers to people who would be taking a pay cut because they are concerned you will leave if you find another, higher paying job. They also have internal equity issues to be concerned about and, while you may need the work, it means you are competing with people who have less experience than you. It's highly likely if you take a job for significantly less money than you have been making you may not feel challenged a few months down the road, and you may become bitter about being paid less than you are worth. Thus starts the downward spiral of your employment there.

Some recruiters believe you should be hired based on your level of experience and expertise, and I certainly agree with that. However, avoiding answering the recruiter's questions only serves to irritate the recruiter whose job it is to gather preliminary information to be passed on. Ultimately, your reluctance to make the recruiter's job easier could make him or her less likely to share your background with the actual hiring authority—and prevent you from interviewing.

Posting Your Resume Online

If you are unemployed, this may actually be your Step One. Recruiters from companies and agencies, both retained and contingency, look on the job boards daily and have search agents set up to notify them when certain skill sets are posted online. Posting your resume will get the word out that you're looking for work.

It is very expensive for companies and agencies to have access to the various job boards, so they often only use one or two. In order to maximize your exposure, you'll want to post your resume on multiple job boards. You may get calls for jobs that are not of interest to you, but don't lose that opportunity to speak with or meet with both internal and external recruiters who call you. By the time you get to their office something new may have opened up that's perfect for you. It's all about timing. More people will work with you if you put yourself out there to work with them.

If you are currently employed, you'll want to proceed with great caution here. Posting yourself on line is a great way to be picked out by recruiters, but it's a guaranteed way for your confidential job search to become public knowledge. Assume that your current employer has full-time recruiters looking for resumes, much in the same way you did your research in Step Two. You can block certain companies from seeing your resume, but your company may employ contract recruiters to do this work. They would not be blocked from seeing your resume and possibly notifying your employer. It's imperative to remember, particularly in times of economic downturn, merger, acquisition, or layoff, even though you may be actively looking for new employment, **if you want your search to be truly confidential, don't post your resume online.**

If you still want to take advantage of the benefits of being posted online and attempt to make it confidential, you should prepare a separate, completely anonymous resume. Upload this copy—that has

NO contact information on it— and insert "Confidential Employer" where you would put the name of the company you work for. The remainder of the resume content should accurately reflect your responsibilities and accomplishments. You should use a private, confidential e-mail address for your replies. Setting up an alias on your e-mail account will help you increase your visibility with as much confidentiality as possible. Most e-mails (e.g., Gmail, Yahoo, etc) offer you the option to set up an alias that you can use for this purpose.

Here's a brief example of how this might look:

Confidential Candidate

Alias e-mail address

EMPLOYMENT HISTORY:

Company Confidential, New York, NY (1/2003-present)

A $550M publicly traded company with domestic and international operations

Senior Manager (2/2005-present)

Supervise staff of fifteen sales and marketing professionals serving…

Manager (1/2003-2/2005)

Supervised five sales assistants in a $10M domestic territory…

It is important that your content is still strong but that there are no indications of your name or your employer's name.

There are differences between job boards and aggregators. You should post your resume on as many portals as you can which are free of charge. Job board usage varies by geography and industry while aggregators sweep the Internet for keyword listings and include jobs that are posted on company websites. Monster, CareerBuilder,

Dice and LinkedIn require employers to pay for job advertising and database searching. Simply Hired and Indeed are aggregators and also have a resume search function available to employers. Ask friends and colleagues what they have used with success in the past and look to your local newspaper to see who they have managing their employment portal. That's a great place to start.

Make the Internet work for you while you are job hunting by setting up search alerts for yourself on the various sites where you have posted your resume. Remember to use a good variety of keywords that include skills and certifications as well as job titles. This will allow these sites to send you alerts as jobs are posted that include your selected keywords thus eliminating your need to personally scour these sites for job leads as frequently.

STEP SIX:

Working With Recruiters

Call them headhunters, executive recruiters, search firms—whatever you'd like—statistics show that recruiters place less than 20 percent of people looking for a job. This is not an indication of recruiters and their abilities or value in the marketplace; rather it is a direct reflection of how, and when, companies employ outside recruiters to enhance their internal talent acquisition department.

Recruiters are hired, or retained, by companies to assist them in their efforts to attract high-quality staff. Companies generally use recruiters for harder-to-fill positions requiring specific expertise. In general, there are fewer available people to fill those positions so they seek outside help in identifying suitable candidates and to make the introduction to their companies. Recruiters can also be beneficial to companies in helping to fill a large number of similar vacancies because a company may not have enough internal recruiters to perform all the research and interviews necessary to staff a considerable number of jobs.

Take advantage of any chance you have to meet a local recruiter in your area who works in your field. You have a much higher possibility of making a personal connection in person and you just might meet someone you can trust and work with in the future. The best time to forge a relationship with a recruiter is not necessarily when you are actively looking for a job; it's when you are hiring employees. If you have occasion to work with a recruiter as a hiring authority, ask them to meet with you in your office. Get to know them. Your personal connection will make it easier for them to help you when you are looking for a job in the future.

Relationships are important to recruiters; the more open you are, the more open they will be. They may offer you resume preparation assistance or share resumes of your local competition with you; they are your best resources for the most accurate, up-to-date information on salaries, job search conditions, and all sorts of other job-related information. Recruiters generally have an area or industry they specialize in and they know a lot about it, so trust what they are telling you, even if it's not what you want to hear.

Remember, most of these people are working on your behalf for free until you are placed. They have their choice of whom to work harder for. Recruiters get paid the majority of their fees after you start, and they have to fill the positions that companies ask them to fill, so don't be frustrated if they don't have an appropriate job for you right now. Recruiters are unbelievable networkers and you want to benefit from their well-honed skills in this area. Don't be afraid to ask recruiters questions. You need to understand their placement processes so you can best benefit from their extensive networks and expertise.

When a recruiter gets you an interview with a company, the most important time you can spend with him or her is preparing for the interview. Ask the recruiter to share his or her knowledge regarding other people who have interviewed there recently or gone on to work there. A recruiter may send you to a company where people you know have worked in the past and didn't like. You should go on the interview, gather your own information, and make the decision for yourself about the company. You never know where someone you meet may end up working in another year or two, and any interview is an opportunity for you to network with the interviewer.

Recruiters place only about 5 to 10 percent of the people they meet and choose to work with. This is not because they are bad recruiters, but because of the industry statistics. In an average search, an experienced recruiter will screen hundreds of people to create a short list of ten to twenty people for a client. Based on location, salary range, industry, necessary skills and experience, as well as professionalism, the client might receive five to ten resumes. Of those, the client will likely choose three to five to interview and only one gets the job.

Feedback is essential for your recruiter to understand how you feel about a job. Just as in the first interview, you want to get the recruiter up to speed quickly on your interests and goals. You'll want to provide solid, detailed feedback about your interviews within twenty-four hours of completion.

CONTINGENCY VS. RETAINED SEARCH

Contingency search means that the client company does not pay the agency until the candidate is hired. Retained search means the company has paid a deposit toward a fee, which is ultimately paid upon hire.

Most job searches over $200K are conducted as retained searches. Retained search firms have a different screening process than contingency. They provide a client with a short list of people they identify as currently available, qualified, interested candidates. Again, this is all about timing. In six months, the list may look completely different.

Contingency search recruiters present as many people as they can as quickly as possible until the job is filled. These searches rarely have a set time frame and will usually be filled quickly. In some cases, though, they can go on for months, depending on the client company's needs, interviewing schedules, etc.

Recent market changes in direct hire search have given way to a hybrid fee structure where a contingency recruiter or agency will take a deposit, but conduct the search under additional contingency terms. This is an advantage for the hiring company because the recruiting process is not a finite term; it continues until the job is filled, often giving the company more choices and a larger list of candidates than under conventional retained search. It also keeps the door open to internal referrals and other sources without locking the company into a firm traditional retained search contract.

Again, the best way to get to know good recruiters is to use them when you are hiring people. Each recruiter will have a certain niche, or area of specialty, and will know other recruiters. A recruiter will also know many, many people he or she has placed or worked with in the past at a wide variety of companies. The longer recruiters have been in the industry, the more influential they are and the more contacts they have that you may be able to tap into when you need them.

When it comes time for you to look for a new job, if you have a solid relationship with a couple of seasoned recruiters they will be able and willing to help you, even if they can't directly place you.

The job search techniques we are discussing in this book are the same ones that a recruiter would use on your behalf if he or she has time to make a marketing plan and market your resume.

Unfortunately, recruiters are often overwhelmed with conducting other searches, so making time for additional research can be difficult, particularly if they are paid only upon placement.

If a recruiter contacts a company that already has your resume on file, the recruiter will receive no compensation and, therefore, can't work on your behalf with that company. It's important that you inform your recruiter where you have already applied on your own and listen to the opportunities he or she might have that you otherwise wouldn't have considered. Maybe the commute is a little farther or it's a company you haven't heard of. No matter what the case, it is in the recruiter's best interest to assist you as much as possible. Recruiting industry veterans are interested in developing long-term relationships.

Asking recruiters about some of the placements they have made in the past few years is a great indicator of their abilities and what contacts they may be able to put into play on your behalf. Respecting recruiters' time is important, so keep in touch, even if they don't have anything for you right now. Maybe a recruiter's next job search will benefit you; or perhaps when you need to hire someone who will enhance your department, a recruiter will know the perfect person. Knowing the recruiter and making a real connection with him or her will make that recruiter work harder on your behalf on both fronts.

Temp, temp to hire, or contract employment is a great way to find a new job if you are between jobs or are looking for variety or flexibility in your job. Contract employment, often referred to as temporary employment, is accepting a work assignment for a predetermined time frame or until you have been made an offer of direct hire employment.

In 2007–2008, the temporary or contract employment industry generated $72B in revenue, employing 11M people a year, 3M on any given day, according to the American Staffing Association. In 2012, temporary and contract staffing reached a new all-time high at $104.8B in sales.

Industry research tells us that nine out of ten people have been temporary or contract employees at some point in their careers. In fact, people employed in temporary or contract jobs may constitute 30 percent of the national work force in any given year. No matter what your level of expertise, temporary employment provides an excellent means to expand your resume while keeping your employment skills up to date. More often than not, it is an effective conduit to a direct hire job, as it can be an easy way to "get your foot in the door" at any company.

Temporary assignments can be either short or long term because companies utilize temporary employee services for a variety of reasons: covering an employee leave of absence for a few weeks, or, in the case of mergers, acquisitions, or other special projects, which may run for more than two years. Assignment length depends on the company's situation, employment needs, and your area of expertise.

You've heard the adage: "There are no guarantees in life other than death and taxes." That's pretty much true in any form of employment; just because you accept a direct hire job doesn't mean that job won't end in the future for some unforeseen reason. This is the case with temporary assignments as well. Companies often expedite the hiring process, creating opportunities for temporary employees who continue to demonstrate reliability, dependability, and professionalism. Assignments may also end early or extend for many reasons outside of performance-based reasons, including head count issues or budgeting constraints beyond your (or their) control.

If you accept a temp-to-hire assignment, it is important to exemplify your dedication to your possible future employer and minimize outside interviews during your introductory period. Employers view temp-to-hire as a multi-week working interview and excessive absences for outside interviews sends a message of disinterest to your assignment supervisor. However, if a great opportunity arises for you, schedule the interview before or after your work hours at your assignment or over a lunch hour whenever possible.

STEP SEVEN:

Appropriate Follow-up

Social graces should not be forgotten in your job search. Don't be a stalker, but don't sit back waiting for the phone call or e-mail that may never come because your application was lost in the shuffle of unqualified candidates who applied.

If you sent your resume directly to a hiring manger, give it a week to ten days and if you haven't heard back from them, follow up. A phone call or an e-mail, if you have the e-mail address, would be appropriate to make sure they got your resume. Then you can ask if they have any questions or if they feel you should contact other people within the organization.

If you applied online or to the website, you should also follow up in a week's time. I know what you're saying to yourself: "Who should I call?" Many names of corporate recruiters are posted on LinkedIn. You can search by company name to find someone who works in recruiting or human resources at the company in question and call them via the main number on the company's website. If you can't reach him or her personally, it's a good idea to leave a professional message asking for help in tracking down the right person to follow up with. It may take a couple of messages and a couple of calls but if you call early or late in the day you are more likely to catch someone at his or her desk.

Remember at the beginning of the book we talked about timing? Well, it's possible that you may be a great fit for a job that sounds perfect for you but, because of timing, you won't be selected. Perhaps there was an internal candidate; perhaps the job was put on hold after they ran the ad. Perhaps budgeting has changed and the job was downgraded or, conversely, upgraded. It's possible that the originally selected candidate got a counteroffer and didn't start, which puts the search process back to square one. Many, many things can happen so don't be disappointed. Just keep track of all your contacts; if you should need to use them again you'll have all the information at your fingertips. Many times the contacts themselves leave the company mid-search; don't assume that because you talked to one person a month ago and you see the same job reposted a month later that the same person is in charge of the screening process. Again, this is another reason it's best to try to get your resume in front of the hiring manager and let him or her help guide you through the recruiting process from behind the scenes.

Thank you notes go a long way in the process, even before you cross the doorstep for your first meeting at a company. Make sure you extend your gratitude to all those people who help you along the way. Just as you'll send a thank you note after your interviews, you may smooth your path to getting an interview by extending a little graciousness to the people you interact with before you are hired.

Post-interview follow up to obtain feedback is appropriate, but don't be overly aggressive. Give it a couple of weeks and then call or e-mail the hiring authority if you can to touch base. If you get no response within a week, try the recruiting or human resources contact. Some hiring processes take a long time and, while it's difficult as a job seeker to wonder what the feedback is, sometimes companies are uncomfortable releasing information about their decision-making processes. You may, in fact, be the second choice in the process. This doesn't mean anything other than that you ranked behind someone else. Plenty of times the second choice gets the job and is exceedingly successful. Again, this is also about timing and who you are competing against in any given search. If you succeed in getting your resume in front of the right hiring manager at the right time you may have no competition but they could be too bogged down in completing internal paperwork to get you on board.

It's also possible that you just weren't a fit or they just didn't like you or don't want to work with you. People are going to hire the person they like the most who is best qualified—which is very subjective. Being overly aggressive in looking for feedback after an interview can be irritating to someone which could negatively seal your fate with that company.

Preparing For The Interview

Say you strike gold and, yes, they want to interview you. Pre-interview preparation is key to making your face time really pay off.

Research the company's website. At a minimum you need to know what the company does, some of the most recent press, and what's going on there. You should also know who their competition is and what they are doing in contrast. You should know what work is going on at the location you are interviewing at and whether or not this is the corporate office or a satellite office.

A job description is a great tool but don't memorize it—over preparing can leave you nothing to discuss upon your arrival. You need to be able to describe your accomplishments and skills as they relate to the company and the position, but be flexible and think logically about your value in the role and to the company overall. Things often change between the time a job requirement is documented and the time the person arrives for the interview, so be ready to ask open ended questions about the work which will drive discussion.

You need to be conversational in your approach with everyone you meet, even if you don't have a full job description in hand prior to your arrival.

Now that you have gotten this far, don't blow it! Many job applicants are so concerned about what's in it for them, they forget that this is the time to close the sale with the company and give them the reasons why they should be selected for the job. Interviewing is often a process of elimination, not a process of selection.

Once an interview is requested, you need to be there on time, perhaps even early. Scheduling your interview often involves multiple people and rescheduling should occur only in cases of emergency. You need to arrive in a good frame of mind and project professionalism from the first moment forward.

This includes phone and webcam interviews. Make sure the interviewer has your correct phone number and that you have the name and number of the person you will be speaking with even if your interview is set via Skype or another video chat format. Phone or webcam interviews are tricky since people often get stuck on the other line or in meetings. If you have a phone or internet interview set up and the person hasn't called you within five minutes of the scheduled time, call and leave the number where the interviewer can call you back. If within fifteen minutes you have not connected with the interviewer, call the person who set it up and let that person know.

First impressions are lasting ones, so always dress for success. For men, suits and ties are appropriate for suit and tie companies; otherwise, dress pants, a sport coat or blazer, and a pressed shirt, with or without a tie depending on the company culture are acceptable. For women, dresses, skirts, or pants with a jacket or sweater would be considered professional dress. Again, whatever is appropriate for the company culture. Jeans or sleeveless tops are never a good idea, even if it's a very casual environment. No matter what the job is, you need to wear good-fitting, clean, pressed clothes. Not too much makeup or jewlery, light on the perfume and cologne, although extra breath spray never hurts. Conservative is always better; no need to make a fashion statement. Piercings, tattoos, and other outward expressions of your personal opinions and creativity are best downplayed when interviewing.

Benefits are important for everyone, but try to save your detailed questions on this topic until the offer acceptance stage. If you spend valuable interview time asking questions about what the company is going to do for you, you may run short of time that should be used giving examples of why you are a good fit for the job. Besides, you won't get the benefits without the offer, so let's focus on getting the job first. Benefits questions are best answered by the human resources department, as staff representatives there have full details about all the plans and how your benefits package will be structured. Hiring authorities may barely know the details of their own benefits so getting the most current information as it relates to you personally is best asked of the experts at the offer stage.

As with your resume preparation, there is a difference between what the job duties are and what the employer wants in a person, so try to craft a list of questions to discuss in the meeting that will give you indications of what the employer is looking for on both fronts. Always let the company representative lead the interview, but be prepared with your own list of five to ten questions about the job, the company, and what each individual interviewer is looking for.

Ideas of open-ended, discussion-provoking questions you can use to create your list are here in no particular order:

- What is the company's long-range forecast/plan?

- How has the company changed while the interviewer has been there?

- What special projects are being worked on that I would be involved with?

- How many people are in the group?

- How would I spend a typical day?

- To whom would I be reporting? What is his/her background? What sort of management style does that person practice?

- How does this job relate to the overall structure and goals of the corporation/group/department?

- How does this department interact with others?

- How can I improve upon the performance of the last person?

- If you have to pick one or two special characteristics that the next employee in this position should possess, what would they be?

- May I see the location of the work area?

- What are the different people in the department like?

- What types/amounts of budgetary responsibility will I have?

- What staff development needs will I be meeting?

- What challenges have you faced in the past that you'd like to avoid in the future?

- Where do I have the opportunity to make the most significant contribution?

- What are the one or two biggest challenges I will face in the first ninety days?

- What are the major projects on the one-year horizon?

- How did you select this as your place of employment?

- How can I show you I am the best person for the job?

- How can I make an immediate impact on the bottom line of the department/company, etc.?

You should not discuss salary or upward mobility in the interview. Even though all these items are important to you, too many questions about what's in it for you takes away from your available time to show why you are the best fit for the job. If you create a solid list of content-related open-ended questions like the ones listed above, you should be able to gather a lot of information about why the job is open, which will tell you if people have been promoted there.

If you are asked about your pay early on in the interview process, make sure you state your salary clearly plus cash bonuses actually paid out. Don't confuse the discussion by talking in depth about your benefits package like deferred stock options or tuition reimbursement at this point. Just answer the question asked. All companies have different benefits packages and while you might be inclined to put it all on the table so you won't lose anything, you may actually be selling yourself short because the new company may have even better benefits and long-term incentives than you have now. If leaving your job means you are walking away from deferred compensation, you need to be prepared to leave that on the table when you leave. You can bring it up at negotiation time, but the initial interview is not the time to get into details like this.

You should be prepared to answer questions about yourself in relation to the job you are interviewing for as well as the person you are speaking with. Sometimes, interviewers ask the same question in different ways to see if you will, in fact, give the same answer. For example, an interviewer might ask what your strengths are, what type of work you like, and what you are looking for in a job in the same interview. The interviewers are looking for consistency in your answers. Your strengths should always be a combination of interpersonal skills and character traits as well as measurable, concrete skills like specific job content, industry knowledge, or computer experience. If you are asked situational questions, you need to state your assumptions before answering the question or succinctly explain the thought process you followed to arrive at your conclusion.

A list of questions you should be able to answer about yourself (and for your convenience, a quick note about what they want to hear is on my blog at www.JobSearchJungle.com):

- Tell me about yourself.

- What are you looking for in your next position?

- Where do you see yourself in five/ten years?

- Why does this job interest you?

- What do you see as your strengths and how would you utilize them in this position?

- What would you consider an area that would offer you growth, or a weakness?

- What changes would you have made, if you could, in any previous jobs?

- What did you like best and least in your most recent job?

- Tell me about an assignment or goal from your last job that you failed to achieve and why.

- What did you like best and least in your recent supervisor?

- Tell me about an occasion in your career where you exceeded the expectations of the employer.

- If you could change or take back any previous decisions, how would you change them?

- Describe the most challenging ethical decision you have encountered in the workplace and how you dealt with it.

- What do you have to offer us that someone else doesn't?

- What are your significant accomplishments in your career?

- What was the best work-related decision you have ever made and why?

- How would your previous supervisors/peers describe you?

- Why do want to leave?

- When can you start?

- What salary do you want?

- Why should we pick you?

- Don't you think you're overqualified?

- What if you get a counteroffer?

- Where did you tell your employer you are today?

Employers want to know you are interested, and no one can convey that information better than you can. If you want the job, say so. Ask where you stand:

- How do I compare to other candidates you have seen so far?

- I'm very interested in this position. Where do I stand in your mind?

- What, if anything, about my background or experience would prevent us from moving forward in the process?

Attempt to obtain business cards from each person you interview with. You'll want to send thank you notes afterward indicating your interest in the position, and having their cards will make this easier. In your note, just as in your cover letter, short, sweet, and to the point is the rule of thumb. You might choose a topic or two that you discussed to reiterate a point, but overall you don't need many paragraphs to accomplish your goal of thanking them:

Dear Mr. / Ms. XYZ,

Thank you for your time this week discussing the open position. I am very interested in moving forward based on our conversation. I feel I could make an immediate impact in the areas we discussed and hope that you and your team feel the same way about me.

If you have further questions about anything we covered or would like to arrange another meeting, please feel free to contact me by phone or e-mail. I look forward to continuing our conversation.

Thank you again for your time, and have a great day.

Sincerely,

STEP NINE:

Negotiating The Offer

The single most important concept to be mindful of when negotiating is this: You need to be prepared to walk away from the offer you have received if you are going to negotiate.

Once you begin the process of negotiating, you essentially are turning down the first offer and asking for a new one. Any verbal negotiation you want to do should be done in advance of a written offer whenever possible. Once the offer comes to you in writing, you should be prepared to happily sign on the bottom line. Don't put employers through the pain of preparing an offer letter if you have no intention of accepting it.

If you are working through a recruiter, you need to understand their process with the recruiter's client. Most seasoned and successful recruiters will tell you how they work and what you can expect in the offer and acceptance process.

How to negotiate: He who speaks first always loses, so ask them what they are considering the salary range for this job to be. Say something like, "Currently I am making X$ salary and I earned X$ in cash bonuses last year. What range were you thinking of for this job?"

This is a give and take process where your goal should be to meet in the middle if the offer you receive isn't acceptable at first pass. Remember – in the immortal words of Mick Jagger: "You can't always get what you want." Be reasonable, flexible, and sensible in your requests.

Most offers are contingent on references, criminal background checks, credit checks, and drug tests. Depending on the employer, one or all of these will be required before you begin employment so you should not quit your other job, if you have one, until you receive word that all checks have been completed successfully.

- <u>References</u>—your list should consist of two former supervisors, a peer, and perhaps a subordinate if applying for a management/ supervisory job. You can also include outside vendors you have worked with on a professional basis, but the two supervisors are the most important. One note: in completing an application, make sure the supervisors you list as your references are the same supervisors you list in the application work history area. If you had two or more supervisors, don't confuse the issue by offering multiple names unless you want to use both people as a reference. If you don't have a good relationship with a former boss, then don't list that person as a reference. Use someone you had a good relationship with. If you don't want your current employer called until you accept an offer, make that clear. You can simply state contact name and information to be provided upon acceptance of an offer.

- <u>Background checks</u>—these can take as long as a week depending on how many counties you have lived in and whether or not the company wants a five-, seven-, or ten-year criminal history pulled. International background checks can take as long as a month. Unfortunately, those college indiscretions, DUIs, or other felony and misdemeanor infractions that were annoyingly painful to deal with at the time they were incurred may now actually be a reason you could be passed over for a job. Worse yet, they can be the cause of your hard-earned offer on the table being rescinded. Make sure you are honest about misdemeanors and felony convictions and read the paperwork you are signing. It will tell you what the company is looking for. These are very touchy subjects, but if you have a conviction and want a better understanding about the company's hiring guidelines, you should confidentially discuss it with either your recruiter or the human resources representative. It is possible to have your record expunged, but usually you can do that only once per county or state you lived in depending on jurisdiction and severity of the charges. If you have criminal charges against you showing on your record, you should consult legal counsel and attempt to get the records expunged prior to looking for a new job if at all possible.

- <u>Credit checks</u>—your salary information is verifiable here as well since your credit score is partially based on your debt to income ratio, so don't fudge your numbers on applications to try to negotiate a higher starting salary. Financial institutions, professional services firms, Fortune 500 companies, and even smaller companies that want to protect themselves against potential fraud may run credit checks. It is possible to be hired after a bankruptcy, but you need to disclose it at the point where you are completing necessary pre-hire paperwork. No company can run a full credit check on you without your knowledge and signature on the necessary paperwork giving them permission to do so. Carefully read the fine print on the application form. If you have credit problems, and many people do, you need to confidentially disclose it to the recruiter or human resources representative up front; discuss it openly. You may need to provide something in writing describing the situation—you may be embarrassed but be honest.

- Drug tests—if you are looking for a job, you should not be doing drugs, period. Even if you are at your best friend's bachelor party or all your girlfriends are doing it at an impromptu party, you can lose an offer if you fail a drug test. Drug tests are required to be initiated and completed within a certain time frame of receipt of an offer, so make sure you don't unwittingly put yourself in a compromising situation while conducting a job search. And just to be clear, these tests are already calibrated to account for secondhand smoke, so that excuse will not likely fly.

Resigning And Starting Off On The Right Foot

Do not resign until you have your offer in writing and you receive word that all references and background checks have been completed. Two weeks' notice is standard business courtesy. Anything longer than that can make the situation very uncomfortable for you to make a professional break and only delays the start of your commitment to your future employer.

This is your chance to exit gracefully from your current company. How you leave will dictate how your former boss and co-workers talk about you after you leave. Don't kid yourself, they will talk. This is the opportunity to turn those good work colleagues into friends. Now that you aren't working together every day, call them to meet for a meal, play golf, etc.

When you start a new job, you have the opportunity start over from scratch on a really positive note. First impressions are not only important, but lasting ones. Make sure you do everything possible to set the tone you want to carry through this important step in your career. Pretty much everyone has said something they regretted in a meeting or wherever in the past. Put it behind you. Don't speak poorly about your former company, boss, or situation. Be optimistic about the opportunity you now have in front of you. Your new co-workers will know you only for what you put forth. Your new boss will make judgments about you and your abilities in the first thirty days, even if your probation is three to six months. Your performance your first year will dictate your long-term success at the company.

Change can be both exciting and terrifying. The uncertainty of a new situation gives way to moments of paranoia and worry. It's not you, or the choice you made—it's just a function of change. New job jitters happen at every level and will go away a few weeks after you settle into your new routine.

Some ideas to consider before your first day to ensure you start off on the right foot:

- Leave home early in order to be on time. Factor in an extra fifteen minutes in case you run into a traffic jam.

- Take proper identification with you to fill out your new employee paperwork (if you have not already done so). This could include your passport, a driver's license, social security card, green card, or other authorization required to legally work in the U.S.

- Know what your exemptions are for tax purposes, and take emergency contact phone numbers for your file. Many companies offer direct salary deposit, and you can expedite that process by bringing a voided check or deposit slip with you to attach to the appropriate forms.

- Dress professionally and appropriately for the company you are working for. (When in doubt, dress UP...not down.) Make sure your shoes are shined, your clothes are neat and pressed, and that you don't over-accessorize.

- Smile, introduce yourself, and treat everyone with respect. Saying please and thank you are the easiest ways to make people comfortable quickly.

- Make sure you have some cash in case you need it. Trying to find a bank or a cash machine in a new neighborhood may not be the easiest thing on your first day.

You will be presented with a lot of new information the first few days. It will take time for it all to sink in. Don't be afraid to ask questions... and be sure to take good notes. If you are invited to meetings to observe or participate, be careful not to jump in too quickly, but don't be afraid to share comments and ideas if you are asked to.

Job change is always difficult no matter how long you looked and how much you prepared for the switch. You will likely miss your old, familiar surroundings. Rest assured, in a few days' time, your new environment will become more comfortable and familiar to you. You will settle into a new routine, develop new friendships at the new company, and still have the good relationships you developed at your former one.

Good luck in your new position, and don't forget to continue to network!

Ten Steps To Finding The Perfect Job

1. Understanding the Process

2. Searching

3. Networking

4. Responding to Ads and Websites

5. Posting Your Resume Online

6. Working with Recruiters

7. Appropriate Follow-up

8. Preparing for the Interview

9. Negotiating the Offer

10. Resigning and Starting Off on the Right Foot

Acknowledgements

I owe numerous debts of gratitude to many people for their support and encouragement over the years. In particular I'd like to thank those people directly involved with the publication of this book:

My loving husband, James, for being a constant source of support and an excellent proofreader.

My immediate family and friends for their encouragement and feedback. For those family, friends, and colleagues no longer with us: you are missed but never forgotten.

Maria Frawley, PhD, and Gail Cato for being amazing editors. Your input was invaluable.

All the candidates I have placed in the past as well as clients who have hired people from me. There are so many more people out there I would like to help. I hope they will find this book helpful in their individual job searches.

My past and present co-workers, employees, coaching clients, and business partners: I appreciate all that you do and have done for me, particularly Lindsay Sellner without whom I don't think I could ever fully complete a project.

Author Bio

Carolyn Thompson resides in the Washington, DC, area and has been an executive recruiter since 1988. Carolyn is a creative entrepreneur and a credentialed career coach. Her articles on career development and the employment industry have been published in various national magazines, trade journals, and on the Internet. A frequent speaker on the subjects of career development, recruiting, and motivation, she is a member of the National Speakers Association, Board Chair of the Washington Women's Leadership Initiative, a member of the Pinnacle Society and the International Coach Federation.

Carolyn is an alumnus of Kansas State University and author of RESUMAZING - TEN EASY STEPS TO A PERFECT RESUME and PROMOTICATION - TEN SECRETS TO GETTING PROMOTED available at select bookstores and on Amazon.

Visit www.CarolynThompson.net for more information on job search, interview preparation, executive coaching and executive search.

Her blog can be found at www.JobSearchJungle.com